CW01665920

THE MAGIC O
MULTIPLES

Twins, Triplets or More on Old Picture Postcards

by

Stella Blazier, Rachel Hudson and Mary Lowe

Foreword
by
Norris McWhirter

S.B. Publications
1990

This book is dedicated to Catherine and Diana, Matthew and David, and Jane and Hannah, without whom we would not have had the interest or the idea of collecting postcards of twins.

First published in 1990 by S.B. Publications.

5 Queen Margaret's Road, Loggerheads, Nr. Market Drayton, Shropshire, TF9 4EP.

© Copyright 1990 S.B. Publications.

All rights reserved.

British Library Cataloguing in Publication Data
Blazier, Stella
The magic of multiples: twins, triplets or more on old picture postcards.
1. Picture postcards, special subjects: Babies
I. Title II. Hudson, Rachel III. Lowe, Mary
796.425

ISBN 1-870708-34-2
Typeset, printed and bound by Manchester Free Press, Paragon Mill, Jersey Street, Manchester M4 6FP. Tel: 061-236 8822.

CONTENTS

ACKNOWLEDGEMENTS

We are grateful to Valentines of Dundee Limited for their permission to reproduce the Mabel Lucie Attwell postcards contained in this volume.

Mr. Basil N. Buckland for his kind permission to reproduce the three Donald McGill postcards featured on pages 6, 37 and 38

We should like to thank Katy Gow, current Chairman of TAMBA, for the loan of the Tuesday Sunbonnet Twins — one out of her complete set of Sunbonnet Twins!

Steve Benz for editing and marketing.

For a complete list of titles published by S.B. Publications in the series, *"A Portrait in Old Picture Postcards"*, write enclosing S.A.E. to: S.B. Publications, 5 Queen Margaret's Road, Loggerheads, Nr. Market Drayton, Shropshire, TF9 4EP.

THE TWINS AND MULTIPLE BIRTHS ASSOCIATION

Registered Charity No.326734

The TWINS AND MULTIPLE BIRTHS ASSOCIATION (TAMBA) is the only parent-to-parent self-help organisation in the UK, supporting families with twins, triplets or more, and promoting public and professional awareness of their needs. Founded in 1978, it grew out of the need for parents of multiples to share experiences, ideas, support one another and obtain information. Today there are over 200 local Twins Clubs throughout the country, meeting regularly. The Clubs involve the whole family in their meetings and activities, holding evening meetings for mothers (and fathers, if they're not baby-sitting), coffee mornings with all the children and picnics in local parks. The most important thing about the meetings is that everyone can talk to people who understand the special problems of coping with multiples, from feeding to potty training, fitting car seats or starting school. One in every fifty children is a twin. TAMBA's aim is to help the children and their families to realise that two (or more) can be 'twice as nice' and 'double the fun'!

An important part of TAMBA is the Health & Education Group — members work in the fields of Health, Social Care and Education, or have a specific interest in learning more about multiples. Researchers turn to the Group for advice and information and parents can obtain advice and support on specific problems from the Consultants who are experts in their own fields.

TAMBA also recognises the individual needs of some families in special circumstances. There is a Supertwins Group for the parents of triplets, quads or more, increasingly important now, as the rate of higher multiple births is rising; a Special Needs Group, where one or more children in a multiple set has an illness or handicap; a Bereavement Support Group for parents who suffer the loss of one twin, both twins, loss as a result of cot death, loss of an older twin, and loss of a higher multiple; a Single Parents Group for lone parents of multiples; and a small register of parents of adopted twins.

TAMBA, realising the need for information, now publishes a full range of leaflets and booklets on the care and management of multiples, and members of the Association have also written a range of books. To maintain contact with Club members and 2,000 individual members, TAMBA produces a very interesting magazine, published three times a year. Further information can be obtained from: TAMBA Secretary, 51 Thicknall Drive, Pedmore, Stourbridge, West Midlands, DY9 0YH (enclosing stamped, addressed envelope please).

FOREWORD

Psychologists and even psychiatrists are for ever telling us about the *problems* of multiple births. This cheery book, put together by TAMBA enthusiasts, Mary Lowe (Secretary), Rachel Hudson (Vice Chairman) and Stella Blazier, helps us to see the positive and even humorous side of the trauma which 79 out of every 80 families escape.

If you subscribe to the view that you can't have too much of a good thing then single babies are good; twins are better and triplets are best. Whether or not going higher than that is over-doing things is a matter on which very few are able to pronounce.

In 1765 the abbot of the monastery of Nikolskiy, east of Moscow, was intrigued by the report that a peasant woman in the village of Shuya had produced 16 pairs of twins, seven sets of triplets and four sets of quadruplets. He sent a message to the court of Empress Catherine the Great. We know that Her Imperial Majesty was mightily impressed.

Unfortunately the thoughts of our all-time maternity champion Madame Feodor Vassiliyev have not come down to us. Perhaps she was too busy to utter them. We do not even know whether she even envied those humdrum one-at-a-time mothers. At least she had tried to emulate 27 times without success.

Her message to us lesser mortals is however quite plain —

"For Heaven's sake *do try* to keep things in proportion."

NORRIS McWHIRTER
Director of McWhirter Twins Limited
Founder Editor, *Guinness Book of Records*

INTRODUCTION

The first picture postcards in this country were produced in the 1890s. These early cards were known as "court cards" and were much smaller than the standard size that was adopted just before the turn of the century. All these early cards had small pictures on the front with a space left for correspondence whilst the back was reserved for the address. In 1902, the "divided back" postcard was introduced so that both the message and address could be written on the back and the front used entirely for a picture. After this date, postcard collecting became a national craze and a postcard album was a feature in most homes. This explains why many postcards from the Edwardian era bear only the simple message: "another for your album". Between 1902 and 1918, millions of postcards were published annually. As well as being saved by collectors, they were a cheap and convenient method of communication. Encouraged by a ½d. Postage rate and several deliveries and collections daily, postcards were used for domestic and business correspondence, for advertising purposes and, in the absence of newspaper pictures, were sometimes the best visual record of national and local events. Because of this vast output and choice of picture postcards — depicting almost every subject imaginable — the era has become known as "The Golden Age of Postcards".

After World War 1, the postal rate was increased to 1d and the telephone replaced the postcard as a convenient form of communication. As a result, sales of postcards decreased and were mainly of the picturesque type that were sent to friends and relatives from a holiday destination. Today, as at the beginning of the century, a vast range of postcards is available and postcard collecting has returned and is now an international hobby, second to stamp collecting in popularity.

Stella Blazier, the mother of John and Matthew and twins Catherine and Diana, now 13, first started collecting postcards featuring twins in 1983, when she was a member of Wolverhampton Twins Club. One of her fellow members was something of an antique dealer, and had a collection of twin postcards adorning her hall walls, and Stella was attracted to them, so thought she would start collecting them herself. She now has a mighty collection, the envy of her fellow collectors! Stella's friend took her collection along to a TAMBA Conference in Worcester or Wolverhampton — we can't remember which! — where they attracted a lot of attention, and were seen by delegates including Rachel Hudson and Mary Lowe.

Rachel is the mother of twins David and Mathew, also 13, and younger brother Tim, aged

12, and in 1986 she was in Worcester when she saw an arrow pointing to a Postcard Fair. She remembered the collection she had seen of postcards featuring twins, and thought she would pop in to see if there were any at the Fair; promptly bought half a dozen — and there she was on the slippery slope to collector's obsession! She in turn showed them to Mary when next they met up — at an attempted parachute jump for TAMBA's benefit at Shobden Airfield — who remembered that there was a monthly Stamp Fair in her home town of Stourbridge.

She promised to call in at the next one to see if she could get any postcards for Rachel. Mary is the mother of Jane and Hannah, twins aged 10, and, sure enough, she found some twin postcards at the next Stamp Fair in Stourbridge. She took them home and found that she kept getting them out and looking at them — and, you've guessed it, after a week decided that she really could not part with these cards, but would have to confess to Rachel that she was hooked and was going to start her own collection!

Stella has now moved away from Wolverhampton and is fully occupied in her work as a Computer Systems Programmer. Rachel, otherwise known as Superwoman by her friends and colleagues, teaches at a High School in Malvern, and in her spare time is undertaking a BEd course and fills the role of Vice Chairman of TAMBA. Mary is currently Secretary of TAMBA, and occasionally does temporary work as a Legal Secretary — when she can fit it in! Their postcard collecting hobby has taken them all over the country, and brought us a lot of pleasure. When Rachel and Mary showed their collections at TAMBA events they caused a great deal of interest, and the idea was born of putting them together into a book when Stella got in touch and showed them an idea she had had about a possible book. And here it is !! We hope that the book is enjoyed by all parents of twins, triplets or more, and by the twins themselves. You may actually recognise yourself in the odd one or two!

All copies bought through TAMBA will benefit the funds of the Association, so thanks go to all those people who have bought copies from TAMBA for their support.

Stella Blazier
Rachel Hudson
Mary Lowe

IN THE BEGINNING....

We decided to start this collection with Adam and Eve — and the cards which make a play on the words 'Pear' and 'Pair'.

At the time these postcards were produced, for parents of 'pairs' the beginning of the relationship with their twins was the birth itself — that moment when the Midwife or Doctor said "Wait a minute, there's another one here".

In the beginning....

Since that time, firstly X-rays and now ultra-sound scanning have at least given parents the opportunity to prepare themselves for the task ahead, by reading books on the management of twins, by obtaining the leaflets produced by TAMBA, and by contacting their local Twins Club so that they can meet and talk with other parents of twins or more. This is even more vital for those parents expecting triplets, quads or more, who probably won't have the opportunity of meeting other parents in the same situation locally.

COURTSHIP AND MARRIAGE

Many of these cards portray the difference between the carefree bachelor or single girl with time and money to spare, and the family man or woman with responsibilities — who face the addition of twins to their family. The additional financial burden of twins, triplets or more still worries families with multiples today. In other countries, Australia and Germany in particular, the additional cost of raising several children of the same age compared with several singleton children closely-spaced in ages has been recognised and additional Child Benefit is given for triplet and more — no such assistance is given in Britain at the present time, although those of us in TAMBA very much hope that something will be done to help the parents of higher multiples at some future date.

THIS IS HOW IT STARTED
THIS IS HOW IT WENT ON
THIS IS WHERE IT LED TO
AND THE LEAST SAID ABOUT THIS THE BETTER!

BEFORE MARRIAGE
YOU LOVE TO WALK BY MOONLIGHT WITH ONE ARM FULL
AFTER MARRIAGE
YOU'VE GOT TO WALK BY ELECTRIC LIGHT WITH BOTH ARMS FULL!

LAST YEAR.
THIS YEAR.

(Postcard reproduced Copyright Basil N. Buckland).

Nora Annie Birch
Why is it when you're single, Married life appears such BLISS? When often in reality, It's very much like THIS!

AND IF I HAD'NT WINKED AT HER I SHOULD'NT HAVE BEEN IN THIS MESS!
HOME SWEET HOME

DREAMS OF LONG AGO.

THE END OF A LOVE STORY.

MULTIPLICATION

The arrival of two babies at the same time gave the artists who produced these cards just the excuse they were looking for to make play with all the mathematical possibilities — adding new meaning to familiar phrases like "One and One are Two — or Three" and "Put down two and carry one".

Multiplication

LATEST NEWS
Matrimonial Arithmetic.
"MULTIPLICATION."

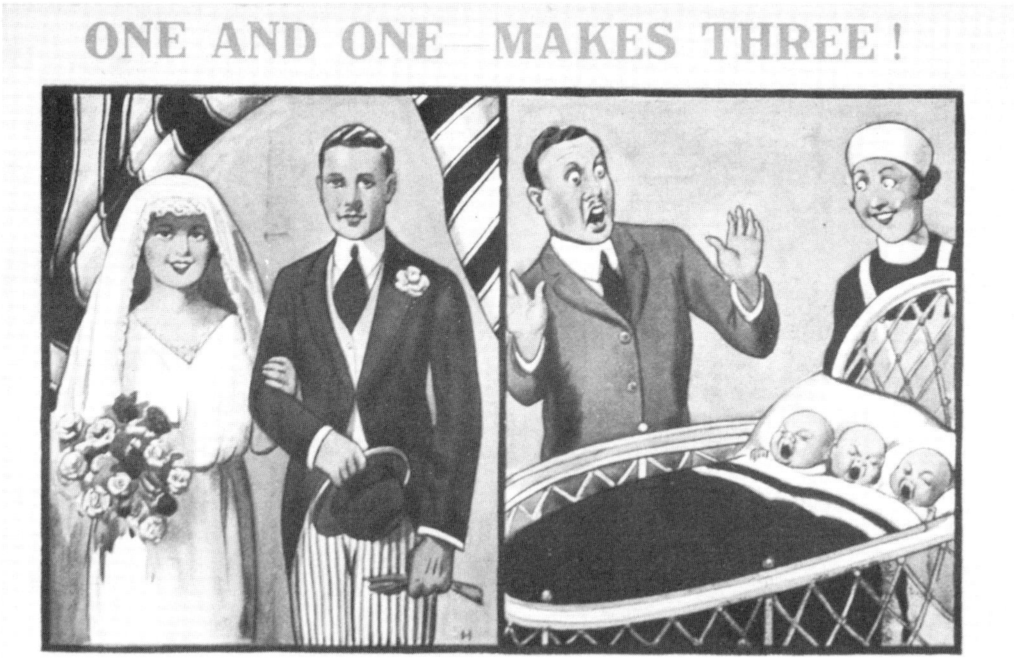
ONE AND ONE—MAKES THREE!

MR JOLLY JOY IS OVERJOYED
3X1=3
86 Copyright 1905—A. H.

NEW ARITHMETIC.
ONE AND ONE ARE TWO.
TWO AND TWO ARE FOUR.
PUT DOWN TWO AND CARRY ONE.

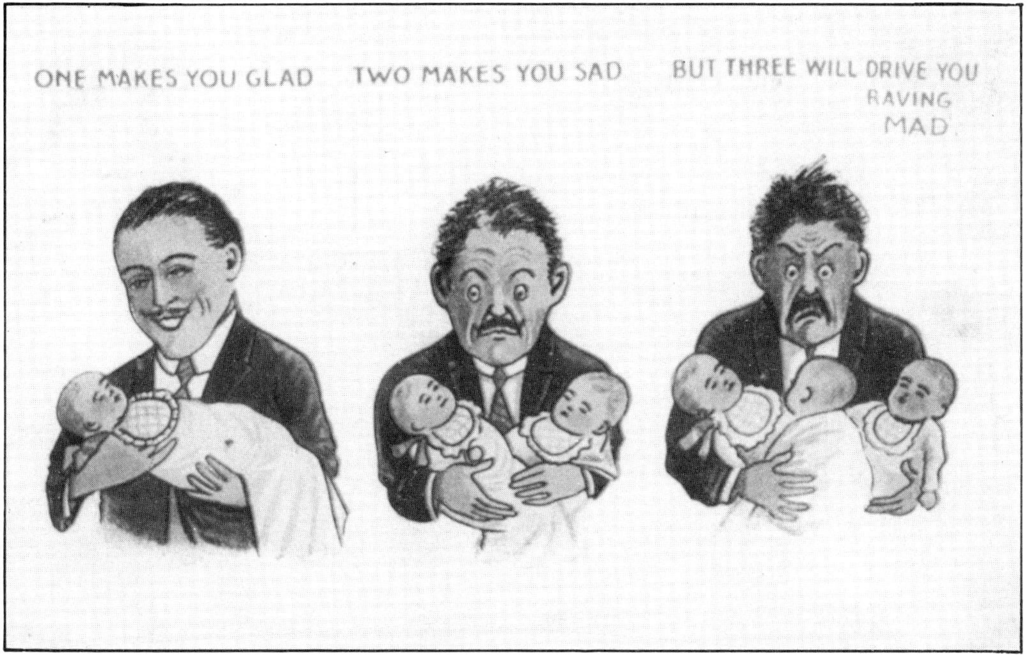
ONE MAKES YOU GLAD
TWO MAKES YOU SAD
BUT THREE WILL DRIVE YOU RAVING MAD.

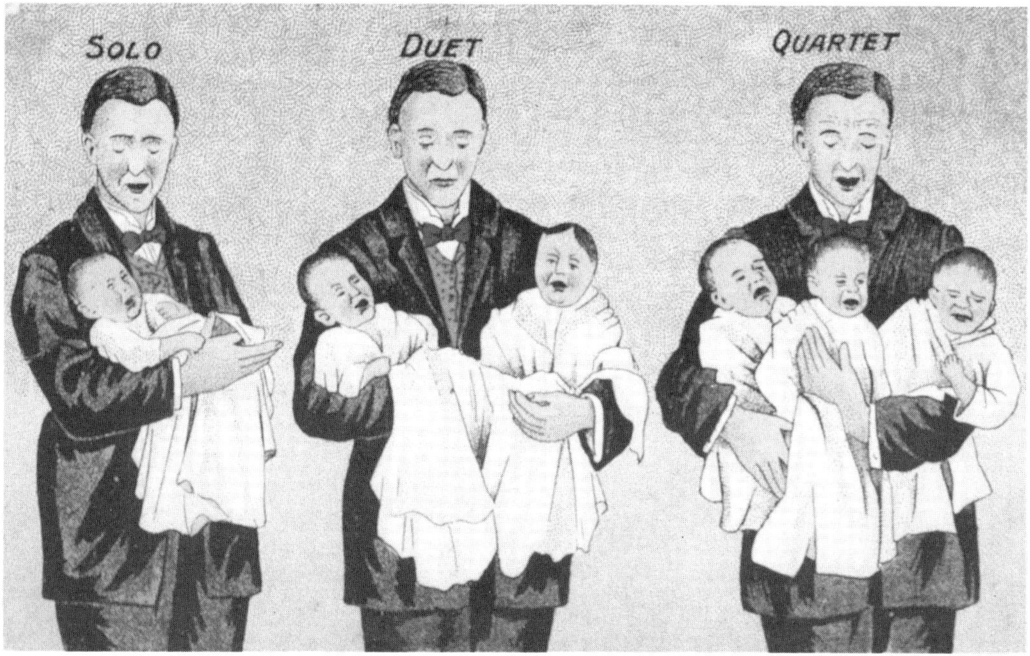
SOLO
DUET
QUARTET

THE BABIES' ARRIVAL

"Come along and bring the children!"

Many of these cards show the parents after a delivery of twins in their own home — common at the time the cards were produced, but extremely unlikely today, in view of the fact that twins are frequently born prematurely, with a low birthweight, and also because a multiple birth is a high risk delivery, particularly for the second twin. Delivery of triplets and quads is, or course, proportionately more risky, and nowadays will always be carried out by a team of obstetricians in hospital. In the past, many twins and higher multiples did not survive their birth, but with the advent of the Special Care Baby Units and improved ante-natal care, many more pre-term twins and higher multiples survive.

Even though parents are prepared for the birth of twins or more, it is still very frightening when they are born early and are very tiny, but it always seems miraculous to parents that they have two — or more — new babies to care for — and many will have a look on their faces similar to that of the parents on these cards!

It seems to be the fathers in the cards who are floored by the new arrivals — we particularly like the Scotsman with his "Gift — from Heaven", who is still standing, and the poor husband in the other card who has taken to his bed!

HERE'S LUCK!
May all your troubles be
little ones

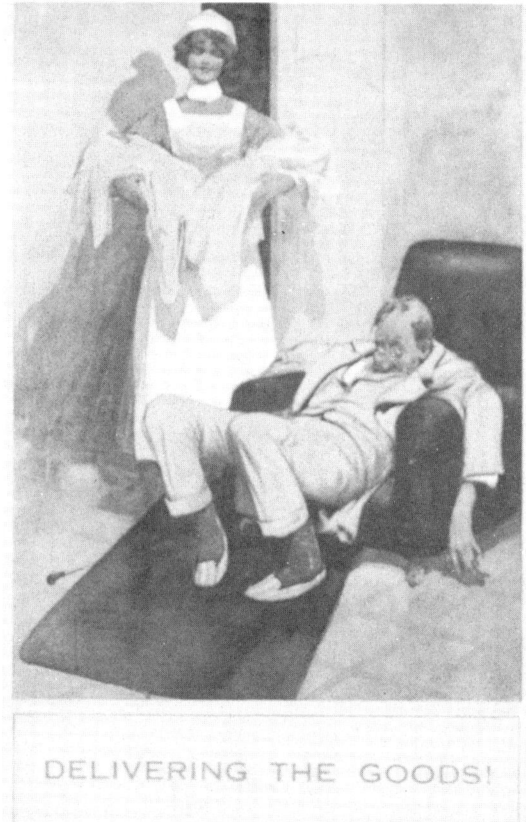
DELIVERING THE GOODS!

A GIFT – from Heaven!

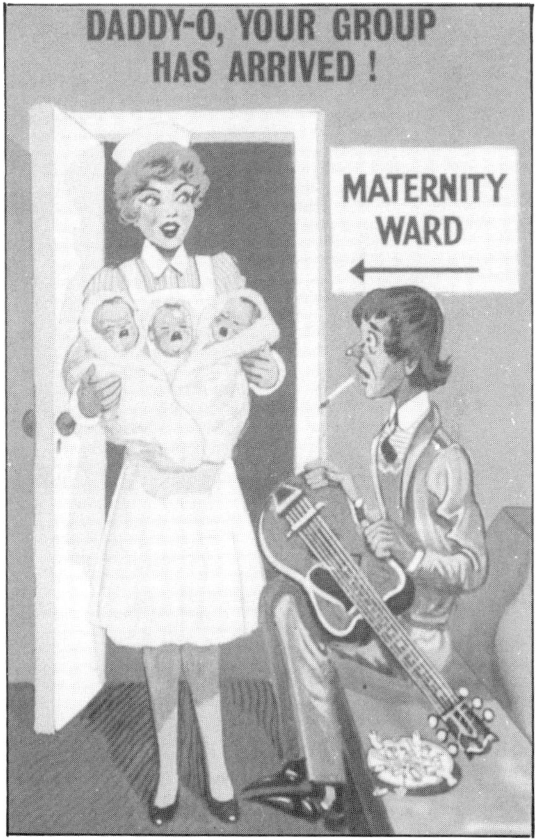
DADDY-O, YOUR GROUP
HAS ARRIVED !
MATERNITY
WARD

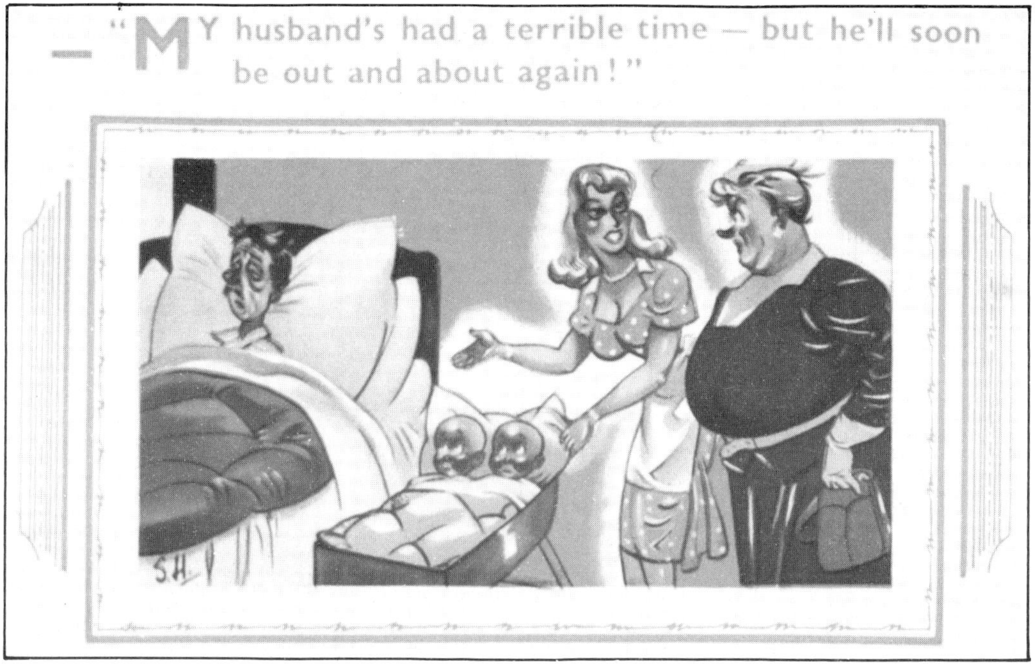
"MY husband's had a terrible time — but he'll soon be out and about again!"
S.H.

THERE'S ANOTHER ONE IN THE
BEDROOM SIR I COULD'NT -
- CARRY ALL THREE.

THESE THINGS WILL HAPPEN IN THE
BEST REGULATED FAMILIES.

"Don't tell her husband yet, nurse, HE'S STILL SHAVING"

WHICH ONE ARE YOU GOING TO KEEP?

This question — usually asked on the cards by a sibling or a father — is an oblique reference to the way in which twins are seen as a "litter" — like puppies or kittens — with triplets and quads even more so. Several of the postcards we have show the bucket of water ready for drowning the unwanted member(s) of the litter! The problem for parents is that, while animals find no difficulty in loving and caring for several young, humans are not accustomed to falling in love with two or more people simultaneously, and it can be difficult for them to feel the same measure of affection for all their babies.

Which One are You Going to Keep?

It is almost inevitable that parents will find one baby more attractive and instantly appealing than the other — and then feel terrible guilt at their reaction, and bend over backwards not to show any preference for either baby! It's important that they relax and accept that it will take them differing periods of time to get to know all their babies — each one is an individual and with time they will come to know and love each of them, and the amount of attention given to each baby will balance out in the end.

SIBLING RIVALRY

The greatest worry of parents who already have a child is what that child's reaction will be to the new arrivals, when they come in twos, threes or fours, and these postcards illustrate some of the reactions displayed by an older sibling. Parents who have already had one baby know how much time they spent looking after it, and they await with dread the arrival of the multiples, and worry that they will not have time to spend with the older child. Many mothers find a solution to the problem by involving the older child in the care of the babies, and making him/her feel very important for helping Mummy so much. Twins Clubs can help an older child to accept twins as brothers or sisters, as membership enables all the siblings to take part in Club activities — and they meet other single children who also have twins in their family.

It is important that relatives and friends of the family pay equal attention to the older child, and don't focus all their attention on the twins — casual acquaintances and strangers in the street will want to look at the twins, and will often ignore the solitary child at the side of the pram. For the single child sandwiched between two sets of twins, or the older sibling of a set of triplets, quads or more, life is very hard, and parents have to try to keep up the confidence of the child, or he may feel almost as if he doesn't exist, and will resent the newcomers.

For the younger sibling of twins, life is easier if they are of a different sex from the twins, thus reducing the urge to compete with these two 'superior beings' — If the sibling is of the same sex, then they may spend their lives trying to catch up, not only with their two parents, who form one unit, but also with the two older brothers or sisters, who also form a unit, leaving them the only 'single' in the family.

ADS. EXCHANGE—WANTED
WILL GLADLY EXCHANGE MONTH OLD TWINS FOR TWO ANGORA RABBITS OR SCOOTER.

Bee
I'LL COP IT WHEN FATHER COMES HOME. MOTHER'S GOT TWINS - HE ALWAYS BLAMES ME FOR EVERYTHING.

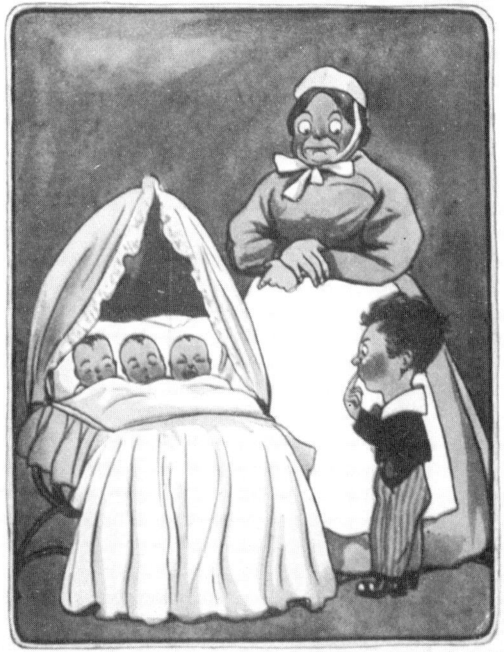

IF WE WERE TO LOSE ONE, WOULD IT SPOIL THE SET?

"Girls! and All the Need for Men!"
"Des filles! et c'est des garçons qu'il nous faut!"

"Did you get them cheaper by taking the two Pappa?"

WHEN I WANTED A NEW DOLL
MOTHER SAID SHE COULD'NT
AFFORD IT, BUT NOW SHE
GOES AND BUYS TWO OF
THEM THINGS.

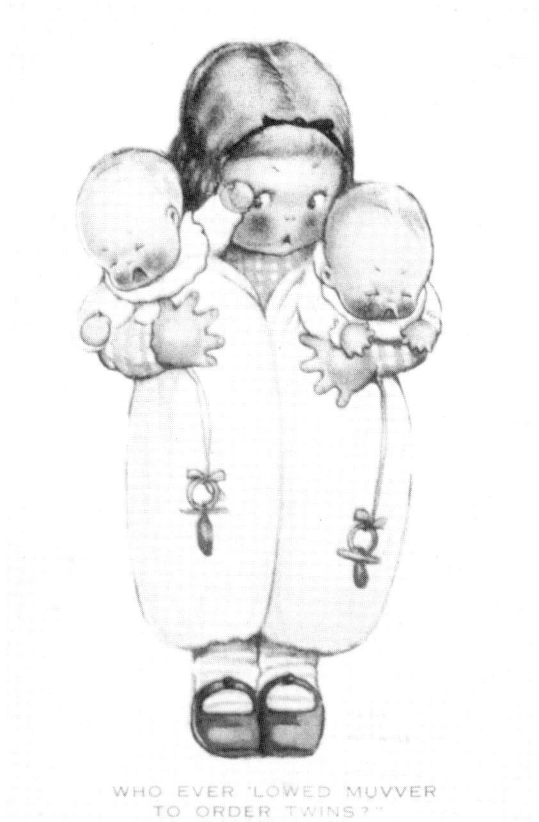
"WHO EVER 'LOWED MUVVER
TO ORDER TWINS?"

WHICH TWIN ARE YOU?

This is the question many twins come to hate because so many people they come into contact with have to ask it — other parents, teachers and the children who are their contemporaries. Of course, it helps everyone to identify the twins and triplets as individuals if they are dressed differently, and this also helps the twins to assert their own individual personalities and develop confidence in themselves independently. Different hair styles can also make identical twins look very different, and easy to tell apart at a distance and from the back — easier with girls than with boys!

OUR TWINS
THE GOOD-LOOKING ONE IS
THOMAS-
THE OTHER ONE IS DICK.

THE TWINS
I'VE HAD MY NECK WASHED TWICE
ONCE FOR YOU AND ONCE FOR ME

We round off this section with a card which features boy/girl twins, to emphasise that not only do twins not necessarily look exactly alike, but they can be of different sexes as well. Nevertheless, every parent of boy/girl twins has experienced being asked if their twins are identical — society tends to assume **all** twins are identical, and that, if they are not, they're 'not really twins'. In fact, only 25-30% of twins are identical, the majority therefore being non-identical (sometimes called fraternal) twins — and these twins will look no more alike than any other brother and sister. Non-identical twins divide three ways — ⅓ are both girls, ⅓ are both boys and ⅓ are boy/girl sets.

"So these are your dear twins! And aren't they exactly alike!!"

(Postcard reproduced Copyright Basil N. Buckland)

EVERYTHING IS DOUBLE NOW

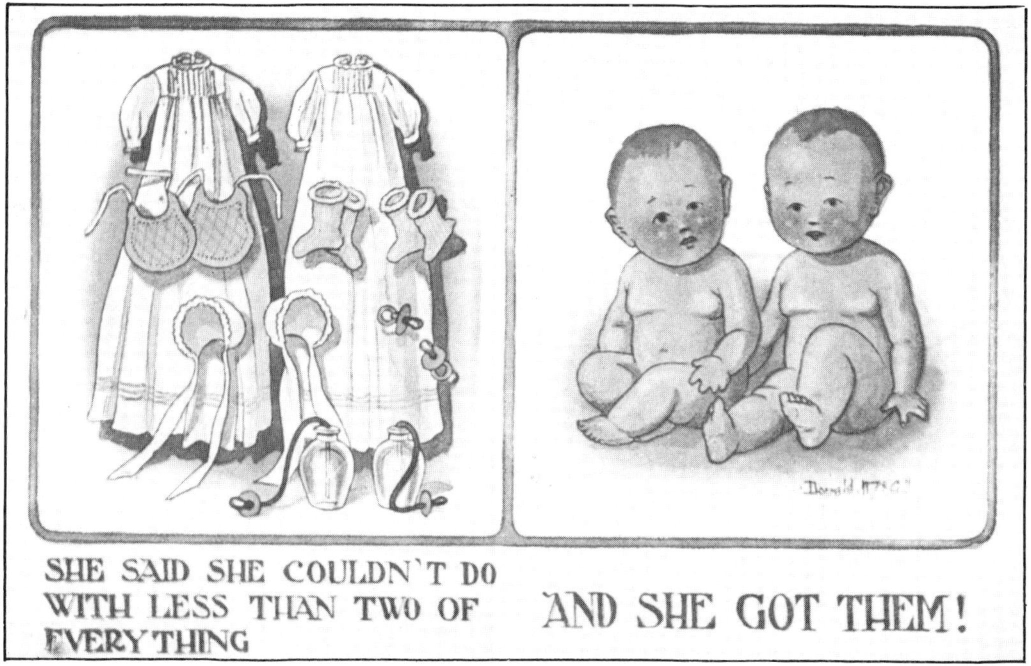

It's not very long after the arrival of twins that most parents feel they are being submerged in a sea of baby equipment — a double buggy or pram; two carrycots; two cots; two high chairs; two bouncing cradles — and then there are the toys!! As well as the outlay for all this extra equipment, there is the question of space in most modern houses to be considered — and something like 60% of all the parents who have twins find they need to move to a bigger house fairly soon after the birth.

(Postcard reproduced Copyright Basil N. Buckland)

Twins Clubs can assist greatly with the cost of equipment, by organising sales of second-hand equipment, as well as sales of outgrown clothes — there is no chance of hand-me-down clothes with twins. Some Twins Clubs have also been able to arrange discounts at local shops — and TAMBA is always hopeful of being able to arrange some national discount schemes. We like the card in this section showing the father rushing round gathering up all the equipment needed for his twins. Sometimes, the outcome of a multiple pregnancy is so uncertain that parents find it difficult to see beyond the birth, and can be quite unprepared when the babies actually arrive and all survive.

D——!
EVERYTHING
IS DOUBLE
NOW!

We are hustling around for supplies,
We really don't know what to do,
One wouldn't have been a surprise,
But the population is increased by two.

THAT'S WHAT I CALL ENCOURAGEMENT!
Sport
£10
FOR A
DOUBLE

"I'm running a little two seater now!"
KEEP OFF THE GRASS

LET 'EM ALL COME
TO look so very far ahead,
You may be somewhat loath,
Still some fine day,
Perhaps you may,
BE QUITE IN NEED of BOTH.

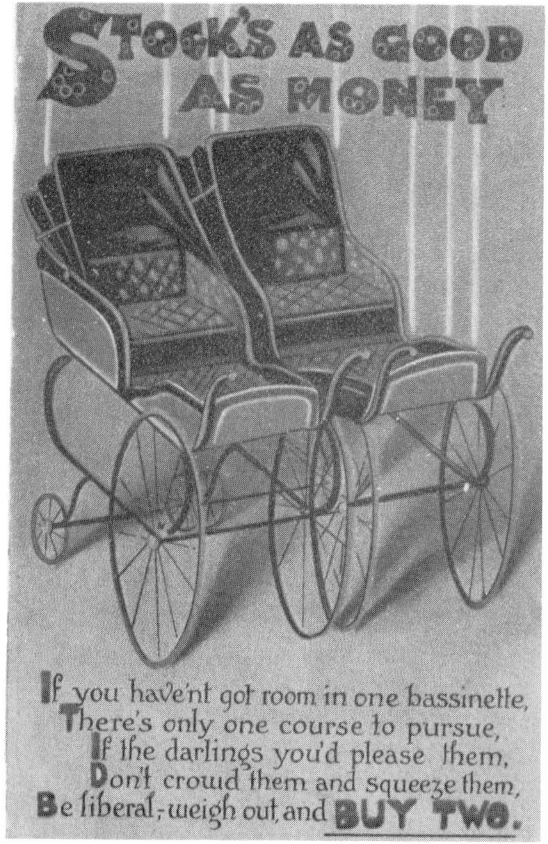
STOCK'S AS GOOD AS MONEY
If you have'nt got room in one bassinette,
There's only one course to pursue,
If the darlings you'd please them,
Don't crowd them and squeeze them,
Be liberal,-weigh out, and BUY TWO.

MARKET REPORTS. ILLUSTRATED.
"Sugar was in good demand."
P.V.B

THE SUNBONNET TWINS — THE LITTLE DARLINGS!

The original Sunbonnet Babies were drawn by Bertha L Corbett and later by Bernhardt Wall of Ullman Mtg Co, USA. We have in our collections some of the original American Sunbonnet Twins produced by Ullman's, and our favourites are the set showing the jobs the Twins do each day of the week — we would have liked to include them all! Space only allowed us to include four, so we have chosen the Monday and Tuesday cards, which show them washing and ironing — both pastimes familiar to parents of multiples — and we have selected two from the range of Sunbonnets which illustrate the hours of the day, nursery rhymes and proverbs. We have found some British copies of the Subonnet Twins idea, with Margaret Tarrant drawing Polly and Pru for Medici, and other postcards which are facsimile copies of the American ones.

On Monday morn with sleeves rolled high,
We wash and hang the clothes to dry.
We help our mama all the day,
We never shirk, nor think of play.
We are the Sunbonnet Twins, you see,
And we are as good as we can be.

1862

On Tuesday morn we iron the clothes,
We flute the ruffles and press the bows.
They're only dolly's things, 'tis true,
But dolls need clothes as well as you;
We are the Sunbonnet Twins, you see,
And we are as good as we can be.

We like the Little Darlings because poor Father looks more deranged with each extra child — and it's what every parent of twins or more says at some time.... "The Little Darlings"!!

Two little darlings! the die
is cast,
Happy they now are, — how
long will it last?

Three little darlings fed from
cow,
Heedless of
mopping
brow!

Four little darlings! I wish
I were in Rome.
Oh why did I get married, why
leave my happy home!

Five little darlings left for
Pa to mind.
He feels his mind is going fast,
so leaves them all behind!

Many of our postcards have a military theme, which is not surprising as they were produced around the time of the First World War, when most young men had experience of life in the Army. A number of these cards make play on the 'Service' or 'Duty' aspects of the military life, particularly the 'Home Service' — where it is used in the context of performing the 'service' of producing a large family — presumably for the benefit of the country. (No worries about over-population in those days!)

Military terms such as 'Forming Fours' also have their double meaning.

PACK UP YOUR TROUBLES IN YOUR OLD KIT BAG.

"CLICKED."

"ENGLAND EXPECTS"—

Gilmour
"SONS OF THE SEA."

I'm on home service.

ARE
YOU
A
SHIRKER
?
Do I look it?

THE MAN WHO STAYED
AT HOME

YUS, FIRST 'TWAS TWINS, NOW IT'S TRIPLETS. NOW ME OLD MAN'S IN THE ARMY SAYS HE'S LEARNING TO FORM FOURS.
REG MAURICE

"Kit inspection? Coo, I thought you said Kid inspection!"

EVERY PICTURE TELLS A STORY.

"THE RESULT OF A WEEKS LEAVE"

WOMEN'S LIB

We start this section with "the New Woman" taking herself off for a bicycle ride whilst Father looks after the twins, and the other cards show Father coping with the twins in various other situations — while Mother reads her book or catches up on the news!

It is true that Fathers of twins, triplets or more just have to become more involved in the care of their children then they would otherwise have done if there had only been one baby — which can have the benefit of making the marriage stronger than before, and gives a father the chance to develop a closer relationship with his children. Conversely, if a husband steadfastly refuses to assist his wife with the care of twins or triplets, this can drive a wedge between them and ultimately may bring about the breakdown of the marriage.

Wife away on
her holidays.

SALE OR EXCHANGE
GENTLEMAN HAVING NO
FURTHER USE FOR AN
EXTRAVAGANT WIFE WILL
SELL OR EXCHANGE
FOR ANYTHING USEFUL.

IS MARRIAGE A FAILURE?
Yes, when you are left to mind the Twins,
and do the Cooking.

DEAR BROTHERS BEWARE, THIS IS LEAP YEAR,
YOU SEE THE RESULT OF THE LAST ONE HERE.
W & A K Johnston Limited Edinburgh & London

POOR PA'S
"DREADNOUGHTS"

"THE OLD MAN WORKS HARD ALL THE YEAR, SO IT'S NICE TO KNOW HE'LL HAVE A FORTNIGHT'S REST AND QUIET!"

MARRIAGE IS A "ONE-MAN'S" JOB THROUGHOUT
OH— CRICKIE
HOME SW T HOME
IT'S A HARD LIFE, A WOMAN'S, SO IT SAYS HERE.
WOMANS LIFE

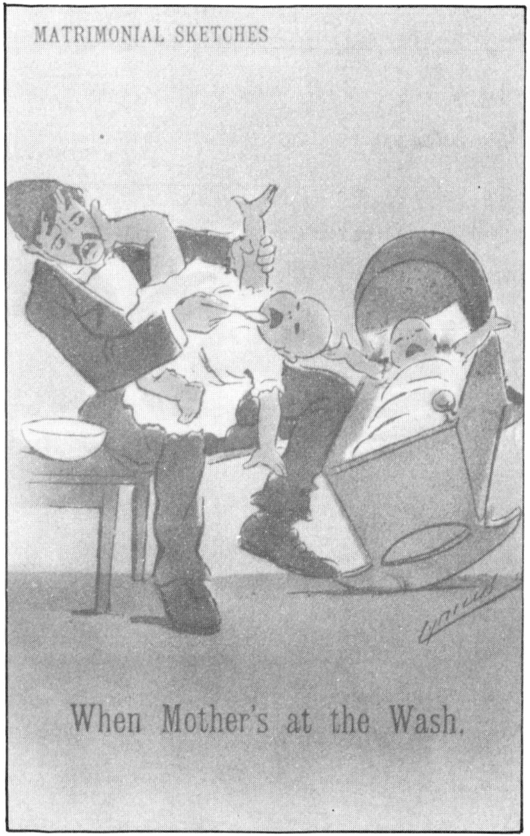
MATRIMONIAL SKETCHES
When Mother's at the Wash.

Subdued

HOME FROM THE HOLIDAYS
HURRY UP! OR WE'LL MISS THE TRAIN YOU BRUTE

We finish with "Votes for Women" — and their menfolk's mixed feelings about the issue.

FATHER'S LIB?

In these cards, Father appears to have disappeared altogether — deserting Mother with the babies. The prospect of the arrival of two babies can frighten off some fathers, particularly if the marriage was rocky before the birth of the twins — two babies can be a rather large last straw! Alternatively, some of these mothers may not have been married to the babies' father. It would be helpful if the facts about multiple births were included in sex education lessons at school, as young girls can be particularly at risk of having a multiple birth, before their hormones have settled down properly — and it is worth noting that there is a higher rate of multiple births amongst illegitimate births.

Some young girls might feel tempted to risk conceiving a baby because they are fond of small babies and want something of their own to love, but the prospect of that baby being twins might make them think twice and be more cautious in their love life! Whilst life is often difficult for young single mothers with one baby, two babies can make it much more difficult for her to arrange for child care while she works, and obviously will make her financial position that much worse, inevitably leading to the babies' being deprived in a material sense — and she is one against two when it comes to a battle of wills!

REALIZATION.

THE IDEAL WIFE

What more can we say?

THE IDEAL HUSBAND

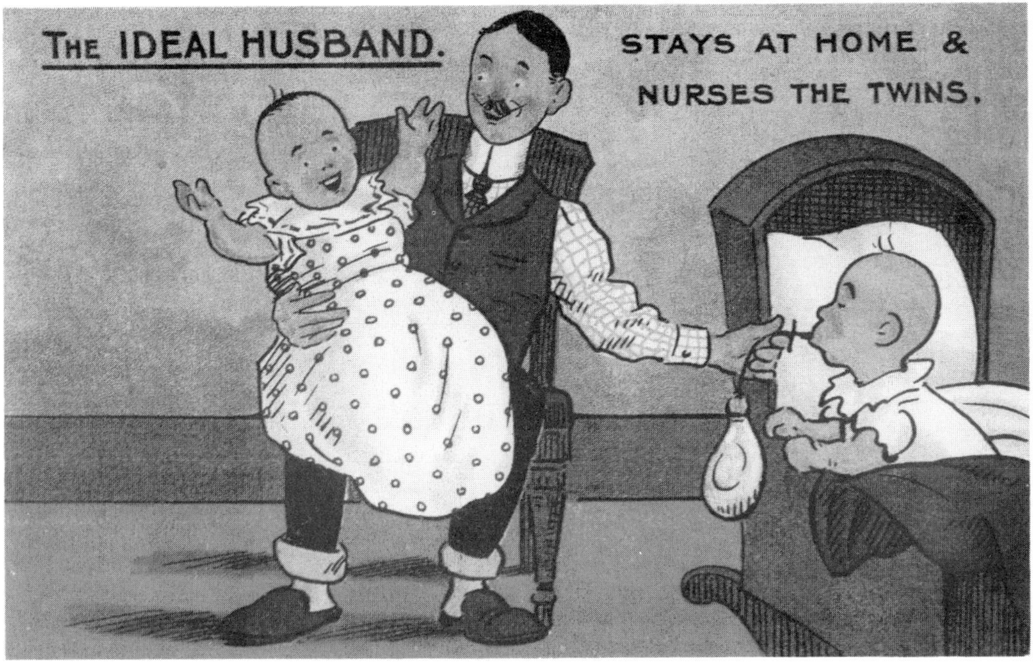

Perhaps the Ideal Wife has gone to the Twins Club Meeting — or back to work?

DOUBLE THE TROUBLE

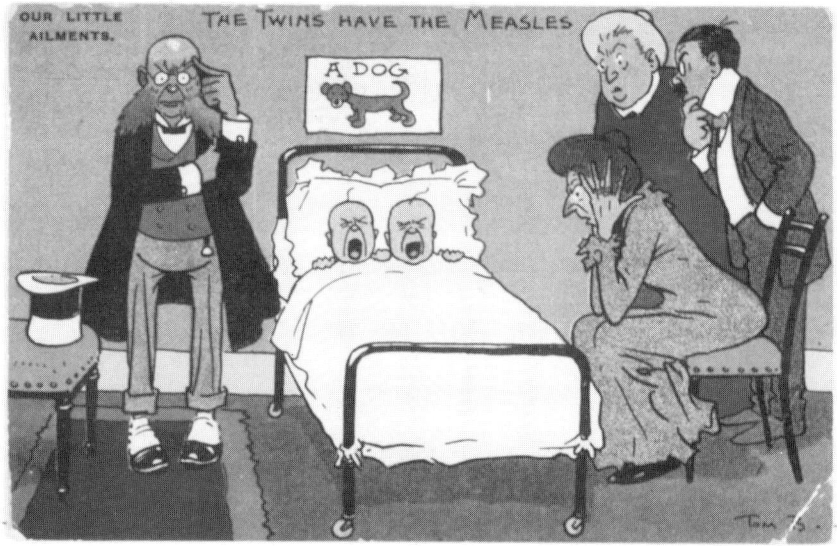

All parents of twins will have winced when the old cliché for twins — Double Trouble — trotted out again in a newspaper caption. However, we have chosen some real troubles — How do you breastfeed triplets? — Look after twins with measles? — Bath twins or triplets on your own? — Afford to bring up a set of twins without a great change in your life-style? — Grab a quiet moment to read a book? — Accept the birth of a second set of multiples? With all these questions, TAMBA and local Twins Clubs can help, if only by lending a sympathetic ear and moral support — although practical help is often given by friends from Twins Clubs, and advice can be gleaned from TAMBA leaflets and books.

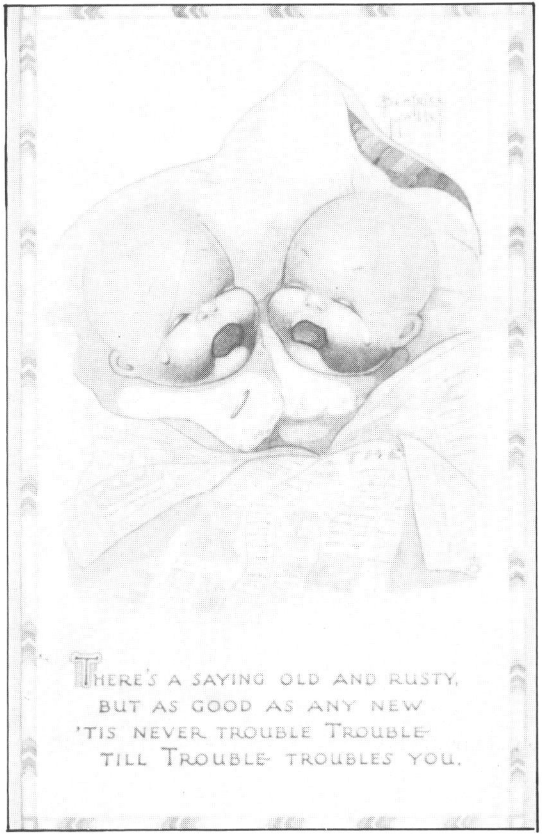
THERE'S A SAYING OLD AND RUSTY,
BUT AS GOOD AS ANY NEW
'TIS NEVER TROUBLE TROUBLE
TILL TROUBLE TROUBLES YOU.

F. Woof
JUST DOUBLE TROUBLE !

"POOR LITTLE CUTHBERT ALWAYS HAS TO QUEUE FOR HIS GRUB."

WE DON'T WANT WASHED WITH TRUST SOAP.

"They grew in beauty side by side;

They fill'd one home with glee."

POOR FARVER IS SELLING THE GRAND PI—AN—ER:
'COS HE CAN'T HAVE THAT AND HORACE AND ANNA.

SOLDIER BOY
A Quiet Read!

Sydney Carter
PROVERBS ILLUSTRATED.
IT NEVER RAINS BUT IT POURS.

"OH NURSE—DON'T SAY IT'S 'QUADS' THIS TIME!"

BUT STILL TIME FOR FUN

This is our chance to show the families having fun — at the seaside or on the golf-course. One of the great advantages of having twins or triplets is that, when the family is transplanted from home into a strange environment, the children have built-in companions to play with with the result that multiples are often very adaptable to new surroundings.

THE DAM FAMILY AT THE SEASIDE
The Dam Slavey
Miss O. Dam.
The Dam Cat.
A Dam Twin
Mr I. B. Dam.
The Dam Dog.
Another Dam Twin.
Mrs I. B. Dam.
Mr U. B Dam.
The Dam Crab.

"I TOLD THOSE KIDS TO KEEP WITH ME—BUT THE LITTLE DEVILS ARE OUT OF SIGHT AGAIN"

"The way they stare, you'd think they had never *seen* TWINS before!"

TWO, THREE, FOUR, FIVE.... AND SIX — THE REAL THING!

REV. W. J. MAYERS (DEPUTATION SECRETARY) AND TWO TWIN BABY WAIFS, WHO ALTHOUGH 11 MONTHS OLD WEIGHED ONLY 6½ LBS. EACH WHEN TAKEN INTO DR. BARNARDO'S HOMES.

We wanted to include som of our real photographs, as we find these of great interest — we wonder what became of these families?

The Coleford Triplets (right) received the King's Bounty — at the time when they were born, it was so unusual for all three triplets to survive that all sets of triplets were given a small sum of money from the King — perhaps this is a practice that should be revived to assist the increasing number of higher multiples?

ROSE, LILY & VIOLET

THE BIRMINGHAM "LACTAGOL" TRIPLETS.

The Mother of the Birmingham Triplets has been able to nurse them entirely at the breast by taking "LACTAGOL."

Rose, Lily and Violet Taylor of Ladywood, Birmingham were used to advertise the merits of Lactagol — a diet supplement for nursing mothers. The reverse of the postcard carries an interesting reproduction of a letter from the triplets' father, saying that Lactogol had enabled his wife to fully breastfeed their three babies — a considerable achievement. Twins and triplets are very often used in advertisements now, with varying degrees of good taste!

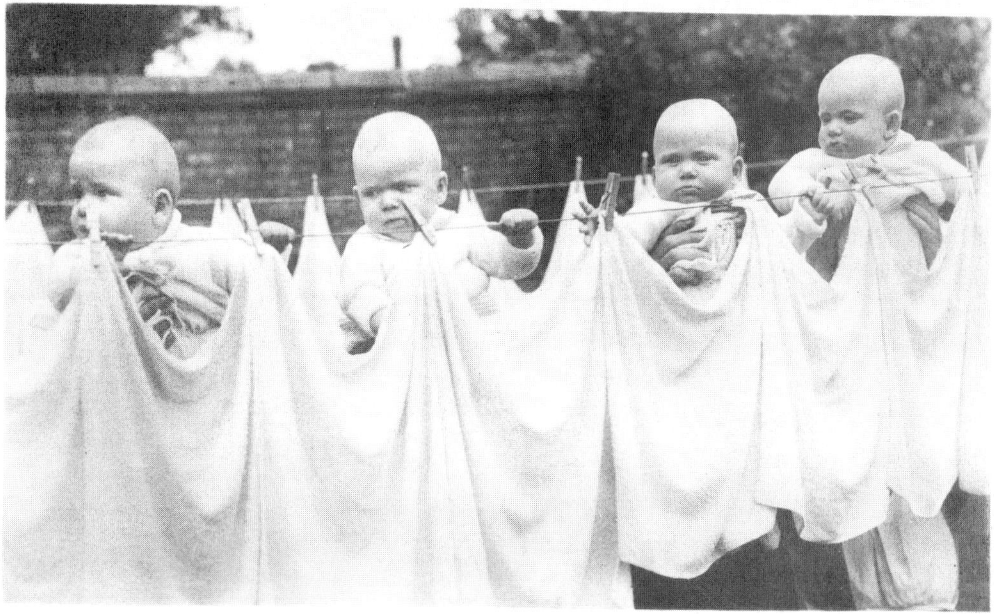

No. 1. THE QUADS. Hanging Out The "Smalls."

The Miles Quads were also known at the time as the St Neots Quads, and we have a series of postcards featuring them and their big brother, with the mother and the nurses who helped in their care. Some of today's parents of Quads would be quite envious of this level of help — there is no uniform policy for the practical help which should be available to parents of Quads and the amount offered varies between each Social Services Department, with some areas providing excellent help and others being very slow to see the need and provide any assistance at all. Extra help with night feeding is particularly valuable in the early days.

"The World Famous Dionne Quintuplets"

Emile, Marie, Yvonne, Annette and Cecile Dionne were born on 28th May 1934 in Corbeil, near Callander, Ontario, Canada. The Dionne Quinns (or Quints as they were called in Canada) were all identical, which is extremely rare. They grew up in something of a goldfish-bowl atmosphere, with people travelling from all over the world to catch a glimpse of them in their home — but this situation may well have been forced upon the parents for financial reasons. In Britain we have two families with surviving sextuplets — the Waltons are six non-identical girls, and the Colemans are three boys and three girls. So far as we are aware, no postcards have so far been produced featuring these children.

THE MAIDS OF BIDDENDEN

Elisa and Mary Chulkhurst were conjoined twins (now perhaps more familiarly known as "Siamese Twins").

Identical twins occur when one egg from the mother is fertilised by one sperm from the father, and then for some reason the resulting fertilised egg splits into two on its journey to the womb — recent research shows that it may simply be a "drifting apart" of the cells rather than a dramatic "split". When this separation occurs very late after fertilisation (possibly between the 12th-15th day) the split will be incomplete and the result will be conjoined twins, joined either at the head, chest or abdomen, or a combination of all three. As identical twins must be the same sex, conjoined twins are always the same sex. Nowadays, if it is at all possible for the twins to be viable separately, then a surgical operation to separate them will be carried out, even if this means that one or both of them will need an artificial limb — it is felt better to assist them to be independent of each other if this is possible.

However, in 1100, when Elisa and Mary were born, this would presumably not have been possible, which is why they lived their lives joined together. Incidentally, they would not at that time have been called "Siamese Twins" as this term only came into general usage after Chang and Eng, conjoined twins popularly thought to be from Siam, toured America with Barnum's Circus in the early part of the 19th century.

Obviously it is a great tragedy and very traumatic for parents whose twins are born conjoined — perhaps especially so when separation is not possible without the loss of one of the twins. In these circumstances, the media interest in "Siamese Twins" must be very hard to cope with. It is worth remembering that this complication is very rare.

THE BIDDENDEN MAIDS.

The following is a short account of Mary and Eliza Chulkhurst, better known as "The Biddenden Maids," who were born joined together at the hips and shoulders, in the year 1100, at Biddenden, Kent.

They lived together in this state for 34 years, when one of them was taken ill and died, and the survivor was advised to be separated by dissection, but absolutely refused, saying "As we came together we will also go together." About 6 hours after her sister's death she was taken ill and died.

In accordance with their will 1000 Rolls, impressed with the above design, are distributed to strangers on Easter Monday, also about 500 Loaves, with Cheese, to the Poor of the said Parish.

IT'S ALL WORTH IT IN THE END

We wanted to finish on a high note — so the postcards in this section all show the happy side of having twins or more — the pay-off!

It is a great privilege to be the parent of twins — and triplets, quads or more. Life changes so much, but the rewards in watching two — or more — babies of the same age grow up together as close companions are great.

We are all proud parents of twins, and we have chosen a selection of the proud parents featured in our postcard collections. We wouldn't have missed the experience for the world!

IT'S NICE TO BE THE FATHER OF
TWO BOUNCING BABY BOYS.

WHAT MORE DO YOU WANT—?

It's all worth it in the end

When upon this event, your thoughts are intent
If to make up your mind you feel loth;
Which would give you most joy, a girl or a boy
This will settle the question
HAVE BOTH.
A Double Event!

"We call the second one 'Encore' because he wasn't in the original programme!"

CHEERIO! KEEP SMILING!!
NEVER SAY DIE!!!

AWARD FOR
"PATIENCE"
"PATIENCE"
I hope as your most Treasured Gift
This Medal you'll preserve it,
And if you haven't Won it yet,
Let's hope you'll soon Deserve it